Praise for *Marginalia*

"Naomi Washer's introspective approach beautifully shows us that literature can be our most enduring and provoking companion. At once poetic and psychoanalytical, Washer's fragmented curation of side notes keeps us hooked on the dialogue unfolding between past versions of herself. *Marginalia* is an original, intimate work that prompts reflection on how our relationships to books can change us, and how those ties evolve."
—Mrittika Ghosh, Skunk Cabbage Books

"Naomi Washer's *Marginalia* made me wonder what books she was annotating—and in that wondering, those books emerged like ghosts. I imagined a book's margins as its hidden spine, quietly holding the text together. I love how Washer illuminates the invisible life of reading, and for how she conjures the intimate, unseen dialogue between reader and text."
—Claire Donato, author of *Kind Mirrors, Ugly Ghosts*

"With *Marginalia*, Naomi Washer puts into words the offhand impressions, half-thoughts, and sensations that constitute our inner lives, that give them depth. Together, these collected fragments reveal how the act of reading shapes writing, or more generally, creativity, but also how it shapes a self, rendering the world legible. How reading works its magic in ways both formative and generative—you just might find yourself writing your own notes around the edges of this searching, beautiful book."
—Deborah Shapiro, author of *Consolation*

"*Marginalia* is a book that interests itself in space both empty and occupied—the marginal space that surrounds text on the page and the physical space that surrounds its reader, who might also be its author. Washer understands that a room's grammars—the colors of its surfaces, the textures of its interruptions, and the windows that illuminate its corners—are responsible for the making of the reader inside it. *Marginalia*'s narrator is this reader: a woman theorized in the third person, a self described in the second, and a fiction slouched into the first. Syntax, Washer underlines for us, is something to be worn like a black velvet dress."
—Claire Foster, Type Books

Marginalia

an autobiography

Naomi Washer

Autofocus Books
Easton, Pennsylvania

Published by Autofocus Books
autofocusbooks.com

1st printing

Essay/memoir
ISBN: 978-1-957392-39-4
Library of Congress Control Number: 2025931962

Cover illustration © Amy Wheaton
Cover image: "Household Lamp" from *Holidays with the Camera... with Illustrations, and an Appendix Containing a Complete List of Contriutors, Titles of Their Photographs and ... Criticism,* published by Hazell & Watson (1891), original from the British Library, uploaded and digitally enhanced by rawpixel, retouched by Amy Wheaton

Marginalia

an autobiography

tear apart your manuscripts –
but save whatever you have
scribbled in the margins,
scribbled out of boredom,
out of helplessness,
in a half-dream.

– Osip Mandelstam

I want to write a book where nothing happens.

I want to write a book that feels like a pile of impressions; a timeworn reframing of a thousand tiny moments; a thousand words unspoken between the parentheses of all my misrememberings.

The references – they build and build.

I know now that I wish to abandon myself so I can become myself; become the written version of myself; transform myself into a book.

Careful: self-righteousness slows down the self-questioning.

The clementine I'm eating has seeds in every slice. They're interrupting everything.

Writing begins in the margins, in unfinished thoughts half saved and half tossed.

Our stories unfold in the margins of other people's pages.

But there are secrets I'm still keeping.

Mistakes and hesitations. Backtracks. Recalculations.

Before I go to sleep, I watch the cars and taxis line up on Seventh Avenue like dancers preparing to leap.

Image of Anaïs Nin surrounded by her diaries.

This is what I'm doing here in Vermont right now.

A theatre of potentiality.

Racing, spilling, waiting to come out.

How does anyone become a nonfiction writer?

Not knowing is what draws me in.

I don't want everyone to know what I'm doing all the time.

I feel this impatient, rushing sense of time.

I need to see and to believe that cooking and eating and bathing and cleaning aren't separate from creative life but rather what allows creative life to continue.

I'm searching for something unexpected to reveal itself to me.

People don't want to believe that nonfiction might be unreliable. There must be something we can count on, they think.

The ending loops back to this – not of love but light.

The memory of the displaced.

The impossibility of the task, the very long process.

I'm reading on my back porch. Red stairs. Blue walls. One neighbor is playing guitar and smoking above while I smoke below. I never look up to see if he can see me, this still life involving a book, a pack of smokes, a lighter, an ashtray, a cigarette propped in the groove of the dirty glass. Now, running water behind the door.

There's a temptation in dreams to become a Subject; a figure that is separate from the Self. It's like a frame surrounding the Self so the Self can be witnessed by the Other. It's like a black velvet dress covering a skeletal nakedness.

I write every day, but each day I also seem to chip so much away – carving the gaudy narratives out of me, sanding down the fantasies to reveal what's left of me.

I always write my passions instead of living them.

At twenty-five, struggling to become an adult out of necessity, how do I feel about my body? After nineteen years of dancing, all the pain endured for dancing, now, at twenty-five, there's a desire to go easy on my body, to let things be simple, and yet there is also the knowledge that I am only twenty-five, that I look much younger than I am, that there is, as they say, supposedly, so much life left.

I remember the fierce, tiny, beautiful girl who was my best friend in elementary school, who did ballet with me but then became a wrestler, and how afraid I was that she would break, become broken, but she was strong, much stronger than me, she used to laugh when we were young and say, "Naomi's so fragile, she bruises when you touch her."

Death makes things more alive – more real.

I've read this same exact story before but by a different writer.

I've never in my life found a four-leaf clover and thus have always believed myself to be unlucky.

The stories we tell ourselves when we are very young cannot be undone.

You were still a child, but the inner monologue had begun.

How many times have I read a writer's recollection of a childhood friend he had to speak for?

To express in another language than mine… true understanding?

Être-là: being in the world.

When you grow up experiencing the intermingling of life and art, can you ever learn how to separate them?

Is it even worth it? How can it be worth it when you have to give one thing up in order to get the other?

Would we even feel more comfortable in a concrete reality?

Sebald called it "the effect of the real."

There is no objective truth, only experience.

Locate yourself within the story.

Writing was always easier than talking.

The winter house is a non-house, like a non-I: what I came to Vermont to be and to have, to inhabit.

Dickinson's aspiration for art as a house that tries to be haunted.

People need houses in order to dream and imagine.

What is a door that is only opened by being closed?

Forgive me, but I don't want anyone to take care of me.

I don't care about "what happened" – I'm searching for the stories underneath.

Begin with the illustration of the concept.

Why I paid a man to etch mountains into my skin.

Or how I sent you pictures of my daily existence: the yellow couch, the white bed piled high with books, the forsythia finally in bloom.

I wrote you and told you to look at the moon.

"Acts of heroism are in keeping with everything I know about you," he wrote.

How to access the universal through the vague and unspecified?

Are all routines ways of hiding?

Reading stories to you in those rented rooms in Oakland, our first few days in California. How you fell asleep inside your breathing. Your body shook and convulsed in turns, always only one body part at a time – a shoulder, a knee, an elbow – until finally, your breathing changed. It paused. It grew deeper, then slower, until I knew you were truly asleep. And then, they chattered, your teeth.

"Find redemption where you can." – Mark Wunderlich said.

Favorite colors, favorite ice cream flavors, and other things that don't exist.

I couldn't fit it all inside the box.

I've always felt ambivalent toward Fitzgerald. I can never even remember what his books are about.

We're required to read Fitzgerald and Salinger in school, and Anne Frank is the required female voice, but we sort of pat her on the head like, Wow Anne, you're so precocious, so many nice ideas.

When one is considered an Author, everything is The Work; when one is not, it lacks legitimacy.

How can we rewrite the narrative if we don't call on each other?

Grade school girls on the train talking about a girl who died and how to pronounce her name. Arguing about the pronunciation, how many presidents they know, how many are dead. How many are alive.

Marriage: the word shines. A wound that gives off its own light. A wound shines.

Moments of intimacy don't need to be discussed. It's a feeling you both have.

You remember the man who approached you while you were sitting on a bench in downtown Berkeley reading a memoir by Paul Auster. He called you Miss Writer because you were underlining the pages of the book so hard. He said, "I can tell you got something extra, something in life brought you here and you got something extra in you, I can see it, I can tell."

We give up meaningful things, toss them out or give them away before we have a chance to realize their significance.

We transfer our love to worthy objects. I transfer my fears of intimacy with people to an intimacy with objects and rooms. I'm the only one who can leave or get rid of them. They can't leave me the way a person can.

My Vermont cottage: a self-imposed hermitage. What does it mean to impose these conditions on myself, alone? It invokes a kind of pity from others.

Smoothing out the creation of the walls of one's home like a bird pressing against its own breast.

This device – what does it achieve?

"Why does this look exactly like the place where you would live?" he asked on that January night that ruined everything. "Because it is," I said. "Because I do."

We link people to their objects. How they survive in the places they've built.

Biography as spectacle. As the first low sky of something reaching…

All these muddy bootprints trampling across the form.

East to Hartford, West to Chicago.

First attempt at creative writing: too much truth.

The earliest essayistic tendencies of children who became essayists.

Corner-dwellers. Corner readers.

A phenomenologist. Or a dreamer.

Show the questions, not the answers.

The question is how and how and how.

To be witness, rather than storyteller.

Martyr means to witness (Greek root), related to Sanskrit root, to remember.

What is the effect of making oneself into a character when one wishes to be an author? Rewriting oneself in order to become an author?

Art is a way of looking/seeing.

Here's a photo of me holding out my hand.

I have confined myself in a miniature version of my images. Must work to absorb, expand, and emerge.

When I hear my station approaching on the train, sometimes I don't want to get off, I want to keep reading, I want to keep moving, consuming movement, the world, this book and this train car now.

I want my writing to demonstrate the ways we slip and dream. I want to perform those demonstrations on the page. I want the reader to participate.

My reader will be called upon to think.

A book organized not by plot or theme but by the singular impulse of a wish.

To live in the real.

To see the world in ideas.

The myth of the real world.

Always, essays live near lampposts.

What does it mean to form a shape of someone in your mind who you only know about from the way someone else told a story about them?

Why did I inherit only these two aspects of Judaism: questioning and revering all things old?

She reveals this at the end so the reader can inhabit the threshold of the essay: they won't see it fully until they too have passed through.

Segmentation allows her to contradict herself and get at the real truth.

Everything she writes is a letter.

The deep connection between the journal and the essay.

The luminescence of objects.

This is the reason you're writing this book right now.

A strategy for providing clarity in a fragmented work.

We can come home to what we recognize.

Consider this moment a checkpoint. Will you feel this way too when you're thirty? So incapable? Will it frighten you that you wrote this to yourself in the margins of a book when you were twenty-two?

This exploration is not going to be what we'd expect.

What would happen if you could see music?

I am always searching for the last note at the end of the scale. Experiments have proven that even those who can't read music feel, when they hear the scale return to Middle C, a sense of coming home. There is agitation and uncertainty when we are left hanging on a precarious D minor. This is why I end my sentence not with "after" but with "afterwards."

She doesn't delve into her own story first, but into the research. Subverting the idea of self-exposure/disclosure. She shows us that it's not going to be that simple.

Start with description. Set the scene. Then pose the question. Then explore.

All these pieces that propel your story in all directions. All this exploration and wandering allows you to place yourself in an unexpected lineage.

In California, I lost my vocabulary. My vocabulary had always been tied to the seasons, to weather, to landscapes that didn't exist in Northern California. I found it very hard to speak to people there, not knowing how to speak or what to say.

It's not about knowing the way but about gaining and utilizing knowledge.

Like the overabundance of literary allusions to orange light.

Or why I feel like I only want certain kinds of people in my home. And why I prefer to live alone than with someone who feels differently about objects than I do.

At seventeen, I scribbled these words on a piece of paper and taped them to my bookshelf: *our sleeping selves form shelves in a museum.*

I don't want to turn into something else. I want to turn back into myself.

This is an essay. How could it not be?

The tale of me and the book, me reading – watching myself read for the first time – and being born blue, and my sister born yellow, and the story of wanting to live inside the colors.

This is how I came into consciousness.

The poem is for us to *enter*, not categorize.

It's a question of previously concealed spaces.

This is why we need both poetry and prose. The poems allude, and can be interpreted in a number of ways. Prose not only conveys but reveals. Without the boundary of line breaks, you surprise yourself with what the mind and hand reveal.

She can't ask about the things she wants to learn, so she imagines them instead.

Like how to be at home anywhere and everywhere.

So much of what becomes familiar was once new.

The many translations of my name, shadows on the streets.

Invested in an inner quiet of the highest order.

The landscape conceals nothing: why should the people?

It was so long ago. I've been so many people since then.

Mythologized = a form of being lost.

(What if the woman chooses to mythologize herself?)

Identifying a lineage different than the cultural one you were born into.

My infant eyes opening on a world. A new language coming into being.

I always want my friends to stay exactly the same. But I want them to appreciate what's new and different about me. I know it's not fair.

What is the soul that longs for that kind of melancholy fear?

She thinks about consciousness all the time, until her clarity sharpens.

She is already beginning to tell a story.

At a loss for language, the world becomes inhabitable.

There's a fear in having the other person close at hand.

The phrase "the faint of heart" referred to someone who was not brave enough to stray too far from the hearth.

We return to the places where our parents lived at the age they were then, only to find out we have become them.

These are moments of attention: ways of re-reading the self.

Creating an author through a disembodied voice.

There are many ways to weave in acknowledgement and understanding.

All these poets always leaning out of living room windows late at night.

Call it *The Book of My Memory.*

Call it *Theme for a Thesis.*

Call it *The Reason-Key.*

Call it *The Book of My Desires.*

The book one might have written.

In my recycling bin: all the notes toward possible plots for books I'll never write.

My left eye has been twitching for weeks. I'm perpetually on the verge of sleep. Writing these fragments is the only thing keeping me awake, yet writing also feels a little like a dream.

I get these ideas in my head, and I don't know where they come from, or why I think them, or why they come to me.

I'd like to learn to see myself more clearly.

I think I came here to see what I could be.

I needed to search for an old story.

In high school, a friend finished reading the book for our seminar before me. I asked him how it ended and he said it was lame, kind of a let-down. "He goes back to the painting and feels nothing," my friend said with a shrug. So I shrugged. And when I got to the end myself, I experienced the same reaction that he had. But that was different than the reaction I had when I reread the book many years later.

I am always re-reading, always becoming.

I often think of Kostya in *The Seagull* crying out in desperation: "We need new forms! And if we can't have them, we'd better have none at all!"

Our lives are not chronological. They are not linear. They sink backwards in time only to emerge in the future then sink back down once more, slipping in between the edges of our dreams.

When we're lost, we return to our center, grasping in the dark. But in that darkness, we feel more lost than ever.

The apartment where Rilke lived in Paris when he began writing *The Notebooks of Malte Laurids Brigge* was very close to my Airbnb, but I didn't know that until after I got home. Another misfire in a series of failures to become A Great Writer like Rainer Maria Rilke. But what would that building have revealed to me?

Who was that person I was trying to be?

Something was slipping, disappearing, revealing a truth I couldn't yet see.

Even when the author thinks she is in control, the writing takes over.

The more she tries, the more she learns.

A note placed in a novel at the right time.

How strange… I was there.

Remember this, Naomi.

Come back to this.

The words we choose are significant.

The words we use have an effect on the way we think.

Years ago, having dinner with an ex, who wasn't an ex then but present tense, I forgot the French word *essayer*. We were eating pizza and he asked me how to say *to try* in French. I paused. My mind did not exist. Words gone. Where is it? I stared at my empty plate. Where is the word? Where is my language? How do I say the words I want to say?

As years go by, stories are pared down to their essence.

Time itself does the work of any student of literature: counting, collecting, shrinking, unfolding, elongating, shifting.

In the hallway outside my bedroom at the writing residency in France, I found a nail and the rectangular outline of where a painting had hung on the wall in the 1960s. The wallpaper had faded inside the outline, the image disappeared, the outline creating an entirely new story.

"Your poem is enough," an old boyfriend once said. But for me, it wasn't enough.

Perhaps I'm looking for someone or something that resembles me.

Perhaps I'm looking for someone or something to wake me up.

Dancing, evening, solitude and light.

I always choose to be beside a window.

Wasn't it always Pleiades I was after?

The emergence of a memory-image is a form of self-encounter.

I loved the sentences I wrote about him more than I loved the fried egg he cooked for me in the middle of the night, more than the stories he told me and our silence as the room shifted from darkness to light.

I need a poem to mean something to me.

I need a poem to mirror something unseen in me.

How can you go back to any of those hazy, sun-drenched, happy times before you experienced a rupture?

What is the real story behind the story?

The story begins, and will never end, with a face at the window.

A woman sits in an armchair, her face turned toward the window.

I watch her staring out the window, no idea what she's thinking or feeling.

But the woman is me.

Is she also the writer?

Why is it sometimes so difficult to be both?

A person who lives alone, or at least in her head, lives two simultaneous narratives.

Is the simultaneous investigation of fiction and nonfiction too confusing? Maybe. But how else can a woman write her life?

I keep returning to this question of how to read her. I want to understand.

She was an invented character who was also herself.

She was the narrator and the protagonist. The main character and the voice who spoke about that character.

Though her work was autobiographical, it was never written in first person and never took place in the past.

She has an obsession with walking the line between image and reality.

She has a tendency to feel manipulated by images.

She often feels as though she only exists in the space between dreaming and living.

The books I like best are the books that show the writer struggling against the borders of her own limitations.

Everyone wants to be a different or "better" writer than the writer they actually are.

We fail to become the writer we dream of becoming.

But those failures strip away our false identities, revealing the shadowy figures we always were.

A character must lose her identity in order to find it again. Or maybe so she can find it for the first time.

There's never only one way to tell a story.

We always leave so many details out.

Sometimes I feel like a background character, though I often put myself on the sidelines.

I step off to the side to observe the scene even when I'm in it.

We are both the actor and the observer in our own lives.

If we can envision and create the fantasies we imagine until they walk around in the world beside us, then we can live amongst them; we can finally be real.

If these matters were simple and clear, they wouldn't be true.

I've written a lot of stories about myself in my head – stories I would never have told to anyone.

Every fragment I write lives in a different tense, or between tenses – between the present and the past, between the imperfect and the future imagined.

I'm always hopeful something might happen. I'm always waiting. I'm beginning to think that's how it will always be with me. As if I had little say.

The hardest narrative to abandon is the one you unconsciously write about yourself.

I'll never be done untangling these threads.

What am I cataloguing exactly? I don't know yet. I only know the action is important – far more important than knowing what I'm after in advance.

What does it mean to dissolve into one's text?

Why do I leave places, even the places I love?

Where can one live amongst the unseeable, the unsayable, in that quiet light?

What do we not need?

Who is the voice who speaks?

Who is the voice who writes?

And who is the voice who exists?

I have so many questions.

Something I've learned about writing is that you never write the books you plan to write. You always end up writing something different.

You wait for the right words to come, but they don't always come.

Lost sentences, lost paragraphs, whole pages tossed out on the writer's way toward getting somewhere new.

I want to allow myself to feel confused and to dwell in that confusion without reaching out for reason.

There are gaps in every story, but we couldn't tell any version without them.

All day, every day, we experience the world inside other people's minds at the same time as we experience the world within our own.

But I don't want readers to escape into the books I write.

I want readers to pick up my books and flip to a random page, allowing their eyes to discover a line that leads them back into the world inside their room.

I tried to forget that room. I tried to bury it and move on.

But maybe I can't move on until I go back to the beginning.

Writing begins from the middle of confusion.

There simply is no time or room for fiction.

Notes and Acknowledgements

Some of these marginalia originally appeared, in an earlier form, in *Sundog Lit.*

I do not remember where I found the lines from Osip Mandelstam included at the start of this book. I discovered them, somewhere, and wrote them down, and carried that slip of paper around for many years without ever looking for its source. In preparing this book for publication, I discovered that these lines come from a work of prose titled *The Egyptian Stamp,* and they appear in a very different translation by Clarence Brown than the version I'd stumbled upon. I'm afraid the version I found is totally unofficial, for those readers who care about such things. And yet, as those lines lived in me the way they appear in this book for so many years, I must admit I quite prefer the version you see here.

The story of how I wrote this book is really a story of where I lived when I read my books. So, I wrote this book while reading books in Vermont, then Chicago, then California, then Vermont again, then Chicago again, then Manhattan, and finally Brooklyn where it became the version you're reading now.

All marginalia in this book were recovered from my copies of the following texts:

The Balloonists, Eula Biss

Winter Journal, Paul Auster

Art in the Light of Conscience: Eight Essays on Poetry, Marina Tsvetaeva, translated from the Russian by Angela Livingstone

The Book of Beginnings and Endings, Jenny Boully

Deadly Sins, essays by Thomas Pynchon, Mary Gordon, John Updike, William Trevor, Gore Vidal, Richard Howard, A.S. Byatt, and Joyce Carol Oates, edited by Thomas Pynchon

I Was Not Born, Julia Cohen

The Body, Jenny Boully

The Beauty of the Husband, Anne Carson

"The White Album," Joan Didion

Still Life with Oysters and Lemon, Mark Doty

"Carlos among the Candles," Wallace Stevens

I Could Tell You Stories, Patricia Hampl

"On the Pleasure of Hating," William Hazlitt

My 1980s & Other Essays, Wayne Koestenbaum

"No Name Woman," Maxine Hong Kingston

A Field Guide to Getting Lost, Rebecca Solnit

"On the Different Methods of Translating," Friedrich Schleiermacher, translated from the German by Waltraud Bartscht

Sidewalks, Valeria Luiselli, translated from the Spanish by Christina MacSweeney

"Red Shoes," Susan Griffin

Bluets, Maggie Nelson

"Once More to the Lake," E. B. White

The Poetics of Space, Gaston Bachelard, translated from the French by Maria Jolas

Japanese Poetic Diaries, selected and edited by Earl Miner, translated from the Japanese by Earl Miner

Walking, Henry David Thoreau

"Des Tours de Babel," Jacques Derrida, translated from the French by Joseph F. Graham

Another Beauty, Adam Zagajewski, translated from the Polish by Clare Cavanagh

Art Objects, Jeanette Winterson

"Translation: Literature and Letters," Octavio Paz, translated from the Spanish by Irene del Corral

"The Brown Wasps," Loren Eiseley

The Next American Essay, John D'Agata

"The Solace of Open Spaces," Gretel Ehrlich

If on a Winter's Night a Traveler, Italo Calvino, translated from the Italian by William Weaver

Collected Short Prose, Boris Pasternak, edited by Christopher Barnes, translated from the Russian by Angela Livingstone

Letters and Drawings of Bruno Schulz, edited by Jerzy Ficowski, translated from the Polish, translator unknown

Hopscotch, Julio Cortázar, translated from the Spanish by Gregory Rabassa

Microscripts, Robert Walser, translated from the German by Susan Bernofsky

The Art of the Personal Essay, Phillip Lopate

"The Task of the Translator," Walter Benjamin, translated from the German by Harry Zohn

Heroines, Kate Zambreno

Alibis: Essays on Elsewhere, André Aciman

Paris, When It's Naked, Etel Adnan

A Lover's Discourse: Fragments, Roland Barthes, translated from the French by Richard Howard

Wonderful Investigations, Dan Beachy-Quick

Acker, Douglas A. Martin

Autobiography of Red, Anne Carson

Reality Hunger, David Shields

Faces in the Crowd, Valeria Luiselli, translated from the Spanish by Christina MacSweeney

Notes On, Magalie Guérin

About the Author

Naomi Washer is a writer and psychoanalyst in formation in New York City. She is the author of a novel, *Subjects We Left Out* (Veliz Books, 2021), and several chapbooks across genre. Her work has appeared in the anthology *In the Footsteps of a Shadow: North American Literary Responses to Fernando Pessoa* (MadHat Press, 2025), *Psychoanalytic Perspectives, Seneca Review, Asymptote, Essay Daily,* and other journals. She is the Editor of "Extra-Analytic: Creative Readings," a column on reading psychoanalytically for *Psychoanalytic Perspectives.*

— also from Autofocus Books —

Duplex — Mike Nagel

XO — Sara Rauch

Until It Feels Right — Emily Costa

Cleave — Holly Pelesky

Nextdoor in Colonialtown — Ryan Rivas

Too Much Tongue — Adrienne Marie Barrios & Leigh Chadwick

Picture Window — Danny Caine

the nature machine! — Tyler Gillespie

A Kind of In-Between — Aaron Burch

How to Write a Novel: An Anthology of 20 Craft Essays About Writing, None of Which Ever Mention Writing — ed. Aaron Burch

Hiraeth — Mistie Watkins

That Spell — Tate N. Oquendo

My Modest Blindness — Russell Brakefield

A Calendar Is A Snakeskin — Kristine Langley Mahler

Culdesac — Mike Nagel

Razed by TV Sets — Jason McCall

In the Away Time — Kristen E. Nelson

The Body Is A Temporary Gathering Place — Andrew Bertaina

Daughterhood — Emily Adrian

Leave: A Postpartum Account — Shayne Terry

Yes I Am Human I Know You Were Wondering — Erin Dorney

A Healthy Interest in the Lives of Others — Teresa Carmody

Out There in the Dark — Katharine Coldiron

Organic Matter — E.N. Couturier

If I Can Be Honest: Selected Prose from the Four Years of Autofocus Lit (2020-2024) — ed. Michael Wheaton

A Revisionist History of Loving Men — Lena Ziegler

The Dead Dad Diaries — Erin Slaughter